Bindi
and the
BODHI TREE

by Ramakrishna Michaels
illustrated by Mae Porter

MOANA PUBLICATIONS

Bindi and the Bodhi Tree
By Ramakrishna Michaels
Illustrated by Mae Porter
First Edition

Copyright © 2016 by Ramakrishna Michaels
ISBN: 978-0-9978810-1-1

All rights reserved. No part of this book may be reproduced or utilized in any form or by any means, electronic or mechanical, including photocopying or recording, or by any information storage and retrieval system, without permission in writing from the publisher.

Moana Publications
P.O. Box 390868
Keauhou, HI 96739

Cover Design: Mae Porter and Kumara Etzel
Book Design and Production: Kumara Etzel
Editor: Ashley Fedor
Proofreader: Mukti Miller

Printed by Bookmobile Craft Digital, Minneapolis, MN USA

I am eternally grateful to my guru, Babaji Shambhavananda, for the shakti and grace he bestows on his students. I also would like to thank Faith, Joanie, Sammy, Pranam, Mala, and last but not least, Bindi, for the sweet inspiration to create this little book.

Aloha!

My name is Bindi and I live at an ashram in Hawai'i.
An ashram is a special place where people come to meditate.
When they meditate they find that god exists right inside of *them*.

All sorts of people come here to learn to be mindful,
but they all have one thing in common.
They want to grow spiritually and to be happy, like me.

Some times at the ashram we sit around a fire and repeat mantra. We say "Om Namah Shivaya."
It means "I bow with respect to the divinity within everyone in the world."
It's always such a special time.
It makes us feel so good inside!

I live here with my Dad, Ramakrishna.
One day Ramakrishna got stuck up in the Bodhi tree and couldn't get down.
I'm a very old soul, though, so when he saw me, it reminded him to get centered so he *could* get down!

Many years ago the Buddha got enlightened sitting under a Bodhi tree.
So Ramakrishna and I hope we'll get enlightened too.
Some day I'd like to climb all the way to the top of that tree!

In this lifetime I was born in Waimea, Hawai'i.
But my family couldn't keep me, so I ended up in a shelter in Kailua-Kona.
That's where Ramakrishna and his friend Faith found me.

Ramakrishna didn't like me at first because he thought I was scrawny and ugly.
That was over seven years ago and he was much more shallow back then than he is now.
He doesn't think like that any more, since I came into his life.
Now he loves me very much. And I love him, too!

Besides, my dark coloring is beautiful and I have the sweetest gold bindi on my forehead.
Can you see it?
Also, I have a wonderful figure and a lovely kitty face.
These days he tells me I'm the prettiest girl in the whole wide world.
And I feel like I am!

Several people live at the ashram.
So does Malasada, our dog.

Since she's a dog, I try to have compassion for her.
Sometimes she gets right up in my face, though, and it's really annoying.
But usually I try to take a breath and let it go because she means well.
Besides, it's always better to try to be friends than enemies.

Here at the ashram we get up very early in the morning.
Ramakrishna and I always try to do some Ganesh mantras in the morning before meditation class.
We say, "Om Gam Ganapataye Namah." Can you say it?

Ganesh is the remover of obstacles, so there is a very special place for him in our hearts.
We love him so much!

Nearly every day people come to help out at the ashram.
They do what we call "seva," or selfless service.
That's when you do work to help the ashram and don't expect anything in return.
It's one of the best things you can do in a lifetime!

My seva is teaching hatha yoga to students who come here.
My specialty is the Cat-Cow pose, of course.
And my graceful presence is very inspirational to everyone.

I love teaching yoga! I teach six days a week.
Also, sometimes we have classes with all Japanese students, so I've learned to speak Japanese!
It's so wonderful to know a foreign language! I'm so grateful for my Japanese friends.

Would you like for me to show you some of the yoga poses I teach them?
You can do them too if you'd like.
Just look at the illustrations of me, and you'll see what you need to do.

First, take a few deep breaths into your belly to get centered.

Easy Pose

Cat Pose Cow Pose

Downward Dog Pose   Upward Dog Pose

(Be sure to do both sides when you do this pose and the next two poses.)

Warrior One Pose

Warrior Two Pose

Tree Pose   Easy Pose

When I'm not teaching yoga or meditating,
sometimes I like to just hang out and watch geckos.
They're strange looking little things.
But they remind me of how many different kinds of people and animals there are in this world.
And even though we all look different on the outside, we are all the same inside.
Don't you love that?

Ramakrishna and I play a lot in the morning and in the evening.
Sometimes he throws me a toy ball and I start hitting it across the room with my feet.
The ball lights up and I love to watch it scooting across the floor. That light reminds me of
the bright light I feel in my heart and all the love I have for everyone in the world
- even Malasada.

Anyway, I'm so happy and so grateful to live here.
I love my incarnation as Bindi, the ashram cat!
But if you'll forgive me please, it's time for my nap now.

I've prepared a little meditation on the next page, though.
I think you'll like it.
It's not too hard, and guess what! If you practice this meditation every day
you'll become as happy as Ramakrishna and me!

Namaste and aloha from Hawai'i,

Bindi Michaels
Kailua-Kona, Hawai'i

Namaste. I'd like to show you a little meditation you can do.
It's pretty simple. I'll show you how.

First you can sit cross-legged on the floor or chair.
Be sure to sit up straight, but try to be a little relaxed too.

Then you put your hands in front of your heart and bow your head for a few seconds. Or you can bow down on your hands and knees if you like. That means you bow to the god inside you. And it also means that you bow to the same god that is in everyone. This is how we pay our respects to the gurus and the gods and goddesses; also to all our fellow humans.

Then you take a nice deep breath in through your nose.
Feel that breath as you draw it down into your heart.

Take two or three nice deep breaths into your heart, and be very grateful for your life and for your family and close friends. And then silently say "thank you" to the gurus and the deities.

Then, just focus on your breath. Follow it in and out.
Just notice your breath as you inhale, and as you exhale.

So just sit there for a few minutes and follow your breath in and out and repeat the mantra "ham sah."
Remember, silently say "ham" on the inhale, and "sah" on the exhale.
Then when you're finished meditating you can put your hands in front of your heart and bow again.
And don't forget to feel grateful!!

Anyway, if you can do this twice a day it will really help you a lot in your life.

Aloha